Lone Star Lost
Buried Treasures in Texas

LONE STAR LOST

Buried Treasures in Texas

by Patrick Dearen

10/09

For Rodney,
hope you find
life's real treasure.
Patrick Dearen

TCU PRESS • FORT WORTH
A TEXAS SMALL BOOK ☆

Library of Congress Cataloging-in-Publication Data

Dearen, Patrick.
Lone Star lost : buried treasures in Texas / Patrick Dearen.
p. cm. -- (Texas small books)
Includes bibliographical references.
ISBN 978-0-87565-392-1 (lithocase : alk. paper)
1. Texas--Antiquities. 2. Treasure troves--Texas. 3. Texas--History,
Local--Anecdotes. 4. Texas--Biography--Anecdotes. I. Title.
F388.D43 2009
976.4'05--dc22
2008036395

TCU Press
P. O. Box 298300
Fort Worth, Texas 76129
817.257.7822
http://www.prs.tcu.edu
To order books: 800.826.8911

Printed in China by Everbest Printing Company through
Four Colour Imports, Ltd. in Louisville, Kentucky

Design: Margie Adkins Graphic Design

DEDICATION

For my son Wesley, my most important reader.

TABLE OF CONTENTS

PREFACE

These stories spring from the land—the Texas soil that gives birth to history and sprinkles it with legend. From the piney woods on the east to the Chihuahuan Desert on the west, from the subtropical marshes on the south to the inverted mountains on the north, Texas is alive with the kind of wonder that has sent men in quest of their own Cibolas for generations.

I, too, went in search, not for gold or silver or jewels, but for untapped tales worthy of J. Frank Dobie. Herein lie ten such stories fresh from the bedrock, shared with me by native sons and daughters who know that the real treasure is our Texas heritage.

Patrick Dearen
Midland, Texas

A TREASURE BEWITCHED

It boggles the imagination: a gold-laden wagon hidden in a cursed cave lost for the ages. Is there any wonder that skeptics laugh, dismissing the notion as worthy of a quest played out only in the minds of the gullible?

Yet for all its fantastic elements, there are hints that just such a treasure might actually grace an underground chamber beneath the Cross Timbers country of North Texas. Near present day Sunset not only did wagons on the Butterfield Trail once ford Big Sandy Creek en route to or from the gold fields of the West, but mysterious caves have sometimes revealed themselves and raised men's fancies to a fever pitch, only to vanish from the ken of succeeding generations.

Documentary evidence paints a bloody picture for this region through the mid–1870s, as Comanches, Kiowas, or Wichitas struck wagoners and settlers and seized what they would. Factual details about the attacks are sketchy, but where history is silent, legend speaks loudly. A long-held tradition maintains that war parties used a large cave near the current Wise-Montague county line as a staging ground from which to launch depredations; furthermore, after the raids the warriors would disappear into the cave with their spoils, which on one occasion included a wagon of unknown origin filled with gold.

Whether the tale was on the mind of a Montague County quail hunter when he stumbled upon a sinkhole covered with rotting timbers and brush in 1888 is not known. But when he lost his footing and fell ten feet, he was intrigued by a set of rock steps continuing down into a pitch-black world. Returning to Bowie, where he worked as a newspaper staff writer, he interested Captain J. J. Waite and two others in exploring the site. On a sub-zero day, as the reporter related in the March 2, 1888 *Bowie Cross Timbers,* the party set out in a two-horse hack with digging tools, lanterns, and other provisions and reached the location in two hours. Descending with lanterns, the men proceeded through the depths for an hour before realizing that they had underestimated the demands of the labyrinth and turned back.

After better equipping themselves, the men embarked on a second expedition. Advancing more than a mile through the grotto, they encountered a snake, suggesting a nearby second entrance, and pushed on an additional few miles before halting for the night in a land that had never seen day. Upon awakening and downing breakfast, the party continued onward another hour before a brilliant flash ahead momentarily robbed their night vision. Investigating, they discovered the source of the dazzling display, a large underground lake that reflected the flickering lights of their lanterns.

But the scene beyond was what truly astounded the men.

"As far as the eye could see, large marble pillars stood erect," wrote the reporter, "a superb, magnificent monument, or a grand subterraneous combustion, no doubt the date of which has been lost in the lapse of ages."

As they studied the chamber, the explorers were even more staggered by evidence that these were not natural formations, but remnants of an ancient city.

"These pillars of marble," said the reporter, "are supported by cross braces and reach in height a distance of not less than 50 feet, standing in natural colonnades. . . . The mind can hardly form an idea of anything more magnificent . . . [than] this remarkable construction of ancient times."

Soon after the men returned to Bowie with their fantastic story, according to a Wise County resident in the 1960s, several teenagers undertook their own exploration and met with disaster—two of them plunged into the lake and drowned. Concerned citizens, determined to prevent another such tragedy, proceeded to the entrance, which they found to be about eight feet in diameter at surface level and sloping downward to a wider opening. With timber, rocks, and dirt, they sealed the hole against further entry.

Folklore, however, claims the men did not stop with merely securing the site—they placed a curse on the grotto that would require a person's very life for ever re-opening it.

The dangerous nature of the cave, coupled with the threat of supernatural retribution, was enough for its location to pass quickly from the knowledge of the people of Montague and Wise counties. In the mid–1960s, however, immediately after the *Bowie News* printed articles about the long-ago incidents, Ed Sisk of Alvord began to associate the tale of the hidden wagon of gold with this cavern. What better match than an abyss immense enough to dwarf a city?

Still, with all parties to its discovery and closure long since dead, Sisk faced a challenge in relocating it. A clue lay in the original 1888 *Bowie Cross Timbers* account, which stated that the hole was two hours by hack from Bowie. Sisk, born in 1912 and an employee of a military aircraft contractor in Fort Worth, may not have been familiar with hack travel, but a northwest Wise County farm owned by his brother-in-law, Bonnie Grissom, seemed a prime candidate to meet distance requirements, and more.

Situated near Big Sandy Creek 11.5 miles south-southeast of Bowie, the 82.5-acre tract lay between two nineteenth-century trails that could have borne a gold-laden wagon: the 1849 Emigrant Trail to California that cut a swath across the territory sixteen miles northwest of the Grissom place, and the 1858 Butterfield Trail that crossed Big Sandy Creek a mere 2.25 miles southeast of Grissom's. Furthermore, the farm was within a pitchfork's throw of an intriguing set of natural rock formations known as Devil's Den, with individual subjects including the Devil's Table and the Devil's Chair. If any location had been cursed, it seemed logical to identify it with a place so shrouded by the name of His Satanic Majesty.

Ed Sisk, *Courtesy David Sisk.*

With his son David, who was only eleven or so at the time, Sisk set out to scour the Grissom farm, possibly with the aid of a waybill he had acquired.

"My dad and I came across a clump of trees," David recalled in 2007. "In this clump was a sinkhole with cut sand-rock boulders in it. A little deeper, there were crossties and other

Ed Sisk at sinkhole prior to excavation. *Courtesy Mike Jackson.*

lumber that had obviously been placed in there to seal it up."

There was yet another detail that must have fired Sisk's imagination. The sinkhole was eight feet across, the exact surface diameter of the cave of mystery buried in timber and rock three-quarters of a century before.

Driving to his job in Fort Worth soon afterward with Mike Jackson, a co-worker born in 1941, Sisk shared his exciting findings and convinced the younger man to join him in uncovering the site's secrets. Clocking out at the end of their night shift, the two men headed for the Grissom place, where Jackson first saw the peculiarity for himself.

"There was a mound of earth with trees growing on it

in a cultivated field," he recalled in 2007. "It's right on the bank, not far from a little creek. You'd just walk up and see these abnormal-looking rocks—big rocks—and this sinkhole with little boulders and stuff just throwed in it. Scattered in that surface were little grains that looked like some kind of a grain seed, and they were fossilized."

Mike Jackson at sinkhole. *Courtesy Mike Jackson.*

The unusual topographic feature had not gone unnoticed by landowner Grissom, a dairyman born in 1920; indeed, his mother remembered it from her days working the field as a young girl. With Grissom's permission, Sisk and Jackson soon began to excavate, clearing away brush and cutting the boulders into manageable sections. The fill between boulders consisted primarily of slough material, but as they worked deeper they found timbers that once had shorn up the walls.

From the start, Sisk's goal was not to recover the wagon and gold but to preserve the treasure where it lay and make it the

Workers excavating the mysterious site. *Courtesy Mike Jackson.*

featured attraction in a commercial cavern. Realizing he faced more than a two-man job in the initial phase of that dream, Sisk offered shares to finance the dig. Failing to stir interest, he accepted the assistance of J. O. "Senator" Lee, a Wise County welder born in 1914.

One Sunday morning while Jackson was in church he heard astounding news: "They've hit it out there—they've found a silver block." Indeed, Sisk and Lee had unearthed a heavily encrusted mass which, when chipped clean, had taken on a sheen like silver.

Already, the dig had generated widespread notoriety—"It got to be a big ballyhoo; talk got way out of bounds," remembered

Timber and rock pulled from the sinkhole. *Courtesy Mike Jackson.*

Jackson—but now all the wild speculation seemed validated. However, with the block now exposed to the elements, it began to rust, and the three treasure hunters realized it was actually a wedge used to break apart rock in an era before jackhammers.

Undaunted, they continued their quest. Below the sloughed section, the men struck blue shale, and as they began to excavate it they discovered that they no longer were in a sinkhole, but in a perfectly square shaft eight feet across with vertical walls that still bore tool marks. Whatever the hole had been, man had done more than merely seal it.

In order to proceed deeper, Sisk and his associates first had to stabilize the sloughed area above. They did so by inserting a twenty-eight-foot corrugated culvert vertically through the section and backfilling around it with a bulldozer. As the dig advanced, the five-foot-diameter tube with inner rungs would permit access to the lower reaches.

As the excavation continued well below the culvert's last rung, entering and exiting became a problem. Welder Lee fashioned a barrel just smaller in diameter than the culvert, and the three men had a makeshift elevator. The first man down in the contraption was another welder, who set up an A-frame rigging and his truck as a hoist, but the succeeding events underscored the dangerous nature of the operation.

"He was digging on down, and they liked to lost him," Jackson recalled. "There wasn't any air down there."

Still, the partners proceeded to bring in a crane, which lowered Jackson and Lee together into the depths. Now they were thirty-two feet below the culvert and sixty feet from the surface, but the hole was far from relinquishing its secrets. True, it was taking on water and there was no sign of a side passage yet, but the shaft showed every evidence of maintaining its vertical free fall with continued excavation. So why should the three men abandon their hunt now?

Forgotten in their determination was that long-ago curse.

Ed Sisk, fifty-four years old in the spring of 1967, twice

Mike Jackson directing operations at the culvert.
Courtesy Mike Jackson.

had suffered alarming spells at the site. "He would exert himself too much and fall to his knees," his daughter Lois Boner remembered. Then on the morning of April 6, 1967, Sisk returned home from work in Fort Worth and died of a heart attack.

Nine years later in September 1976, Lee also would die.

The stunning developments not only ended the quest for

The crane at work at the dig site. *Courtesy Mike Jackson.*

a mystery, but launched Sisk's son David on a vain search for answers of his own. "They said that somebody put a curse on it—that if you tried to open that cave up, then you would die," he reflected in 2007. "I don't know anything about that, but my dad and J. O. 'Senator' Lee both died after trying to open the cave."

For two decades after Sisk's death, the site languished in oblivion, as Jackson pursued other goals. Not until 1986 did he regain interest with the encouragement of a friend from Weatherford. The property had long since changed hands, but Jackson negotiated an agreement with the new owner and resumed his investigation. His most ambitious endeavor came in 1991 when he commissioned a magnetic search of the shaft and vicinity by R. M. Herzfeld of Dallas. Herzfeld fittingly dubbed the operation the Cibola Project, commemorating Spanish conquistadors' pursuit of a fabled city of gold.

"From the data, there definitely appears to be a very anomalous area just to the north of the shaft," Herzfeld reported on July 11, 1991. "The magnetic measurements are displaying a concentration of low readings, which could indicate a void in the subsurface. . . . The strongest intensity [is] at approximately 400 feet north-northwest of the shaft." Jackson later indicated that this was a typographical error and that the actual distance was forty feet.

Although depth projections in non-magnetic areas such as caverns were problematic, Herzfeld calculated from the electrical data that the void lay sixty to ninety feet below the surface. After the geophysicist staked the boundaries, Jackson and his new partner core-drilled the area, but failed to locate a horizontal passage veering from the shaft as Sisk had always believed to exist.

Jackson, the only survivor of the original threesome, finally gave up the search, though the haunting questions lingered in his mind well into the twenty-first century.

"That was a very peculiar experience that I went through with that, and I've always wondered," he reflected in 2007. "I don't guess I'll ever know what it was."

Meanwhile, the wagon and its golden load still lie hidden, whether in a cursed cavern passage a little north of a water-filled shaft, or merely in a century-plus of folklore, no one can say. The only thing certain is that men go and come, but treasures abide. ★

OUTLAW GOLD ON THE SAN GABRIEL

Mahomet was a sleepy town, especially in the late 1930s. Hugging the North Fork of the San Gabriel River at an elevation of 1,030 feet in eastern Burnet County forty miles northwest of Austin, the farming community boasted of only forty residents, a tabernacle, and a combination gas station-store where folks gathered to swig soda pop, play dominoes, and chew the fat.

Mahomet Store during the Great Depression.
Courtesy Geraldine Booth.

Little did they know that they were about to bear witness to a legend.

When one elderly gent, a newcomer whose name has escaped history, shuffled in with a wild tale of armed robbery, flight, and buried treasure, the store's patrons didn't know what to make of him. But in between games of dominoes, they listened, nodded, and humored the old-timer.

Stories of bank and train heists were nothing new in Mahomet. Not half a mile away lay the grave of William Henry Whitley, who had bossed a gang of robbers until lawmen gunned him down in Floresville soon after his twenty-fourth birthday in 1888. Even now, a Mahomet tree bore a carving by the outlaw's own hand. But a generation had passed since Whitley's daring exploits, long enough for the stranger's story to take on a fresh sheen, particularly to the young boys whose only entertainment had been to prowl the oaks that cloaked the river and tributaries.

Even as the old fellow assimilated into the community and his story floated from household to household, no one realized that his quest for hidden loot neared a climax. Then one day he approached Billie Joe Goble, who was about ten, and a couple of other boys to assist in his search. As they wandered the snaking water courses, the excitement loosened the old man's tongue and the youngsters heard the full details of an incredible tale that set their blood pounding.

The parallels with Whitley and his gang are striking.

In the old-timer's youth, which must have been in the 1800s, the man had strayed from the straight and narrow and joined a band of outlaws. He didn't hesitate when they turned

to armed robbery and struck a Texas town, but he had second thoughts as they fled horseback with a posse on their rump. Still, they carried the fruits of their crime, enough gold for all of them to live in ease the rest of their lives.

That is, if they survived.

Dodging bullets, the gang reached the San Gabriel's north fork and pulled rein an uncomfortable distance ahead of the lawmen. Perhaps the weight of the gold slowed their mounts, or maybe they realized escape was impossible regardless and therefore planned for the future. At any rate, they killed a horse, wrapped their spoils in the hide, and buried it near one tree among thousands.

Billie Joe Goble.
Courtesy Carol Goble.

Taking aim with their six-shooters, they pumped slug after slug into the bark, marking it in true outlaw fashion.

Pushing on desperately, the bandits came under fire and suffered casualties before the posse rode them down and captured the survivors. Their misdeed and refusal to reveal the money's whereabouts netted the men harsh sentences, and only one of them outlived his stay in the crossbar hotel. Now he had returned, in the twilight of his years, to seize the loot that had cost him so much.

Scouring the thickets, Billie Joe and his friends discovered a tree bearing long-ago scars and set to work to determine the veracity of the old man's words.

"Dad said they dug lead slugs out of the tree with their pocketknives," related Billie Joe's son, Perry Goble, in 2007. "He said that it had been shot."

With their excitement at a fever pitch, the boys sank hole after hole in the surrounding ground at the onetime outlaw's bidding,

Billie Joe Goble.
Courtesy Carol Goble.

but the horsehide and gold stayed hidden, and remain so to this day.

Billie Joe carried the memory of that 1930s quest on into 2000 when he died at age seventy-one, but the questions linger. Was there any truth to the old fellow's story? Had he indeed been part of a robbery and helped conceal the swag so well that not even he had been able to relocate it? Even more intriguing, might he have been a member of the Whitley gang of documented history? After all, rumors of buried loot had generated searches on the old Whitley place along Lucy Creek thirty miles northwest of Mahomet since the 1890s.

Two opposite schools of thought either dash the treasure hunter's hopes or elevate them to extraordinary heights.

"The old man was either confiding in these boys to help him hunt and to help him dig," assessed Perry Goble, "or he was just having fun with them. Who knows?"

Maybe the answers still lie hidden beneath a stately old tree in a sleepy Central Texas town. ★

COMANCHE JEWELS

Up a bloody trace through Texas they rode for a hundred years—Comanches returning from Mexico with spoils that once may have included a fabulous treasure now hidden in Stephens County.

Early on, these Indians from the Arkansas and Red rivers learned the value that the white man placed on things jeweled or glittering, so when warriors reportedly seized a fortune in rubies and other valuables on a mid-1800s raid in Mexico, they knew it could bring them guns and powder. Turning back for Texas, they splashed their horses across the Rio Grande in the Big Bend and pressed on for the distant Clear Fork of the Brazos and its tributary, Hubbard Creek. In broken country a few miles northwest of Hubbard, a white man and his Comanche wife welcomed the band at their dugout and two-room box house with cistern, the most isolated of homesteads in an area without Anglo settlement until 1857.

The warriors had been this way before. Indeed, the white man often had taken their booty to east-lying settlements and exchanged it for items the Indians could utilize. Already, he had buried a five-year-old girl under a nearby oak, and he would do what he must to keep his surviving ward, a young niece, from meeting the same fate. Now, as warriors followed them inside and dumped a veritable treasure on the table, the prospects for trade were astounding.

The little girl looked on wide-eyed, never having dreamed of such a bonanza. With the Comanches' permission, her uncle

A Comanche Warrior, by Frederic Remington. *Library of Congress.*

took a ruby as large as a quail egg from the pile and gave it to her. The rest, they took outside and concealed in a tunnel as always, pending such time as the white man could venture to the settlements. The girl was not allowed to accompany them to the cache, but she already had taken note that they invariably returned within ten or fifteen minutes.

Evidently to guard against the unexpected deaths of all who knew its location, her uncle soon fashioned an antelope-hide map. For reasons unknown, he never exchanged the treasure for goods; perhaps his fears of everyone's sudden demise were realized. At any rate, the niece alone came into possession of the parchment and, in old age, bequeathed it to her great-grandson and told him of the jeweled cache.

By the early 1930s, the dugout and box house were but lonely monuments eleven miles northwest of Breckenridge on the ranch of William Henry Green, who had founded the spread as an eighteen-year-old in 1886. His son Bob, born in 1924, was only a boy of eight or ten when a man named Smith showed up one day at the Greens' backyard gate. The proprietor of a junkyard in Odessa, this stranger with the nickname "Smitty" flashed a map, related the story told him by his great-grandmother, and asked permission to dig at the old homestead. A one-quarter share of whatever he found would go to the rancher.

Although William Henry had noticed half-circles etched in rock near the location, the tale was new

William Henry Green.
Courtesy Bob Green.

21

to him. Regardless, the proposition seemed sound. "That's a lot more than the oil people would give me," he observed. "Go ahead."

Smitty made camp near the old homestead, and his crew of shareholders began to dig, hoisting dirt from the depths with a barrel and tackle powered by an old car engine. The laborers soon learned to gouge niches in the wall as shelters, for the apparatus was prone to collapsing. Still, it was effective.

"They would dig some of the damnedest holes you ever saw—ten foot across and forty foot deep," remembered Bob Green, who was destined to share many seasons with Smitty. "We'd fill the holes in with a bulldozer so our cattle wouldn't fall in. And then he'd come back the next year and he'd refigured and sometimes he'd say, 'I didn't dig four foot deep enough,' and he'd dig it all out again."

Smitty based his calculations not only on the antelope hide, which stayed locked in a safe at home, but on a map sketched on a scroll of wallpaper. Even with this working map, he was discreet, and the younger Green could glimpse only circles, stars, and scrawls before the treasure hunter would quickly roll it up again.

"Now a lot of this stuff on here don't mean nothing," Smitty once told him when he let the rancher's gaze linger too long. "I'm the only one knows what means anything."

As he returned year after year in quest of the long-lost cache, Smitty faced his share of setbacks. Once, disenchanted shareholders assaulted him. Another time, a grass fire roared across the range and he could find no escape, except down. When the rancher later checked on his welfare, he learned that

Smitty had ridden out the fire storm from the bottom of his latest hole.

Nevertheless, the junkyard owner stayed determined, buoyed by a zeal born of his great-grandmother's testimony.

"He could really fill you full if you'd listen," Bob Green recalled. "He made an awful good story out of it—he kept adding to it. I'd tell people about it and they'd say, 'Aw, is that really so?' We'd drive over there and by the time he got through with them, they'd have a shovel and be digging."

One day Green found him chiseling through a five-foot-thick rock formation dating to the dinosaur age. "Seems unlikely you'd find any treasure beneath *that*," the rancher offered.

Smitty was far from dismayed. "Them Indians was awful crafty," he contended.

On another occasion, the Odessan announced to the rancher that his calculations indicated the jewels were buried beneath the two-room box house. "Would you care if I took the

Bob Green. *Courtesy Bob Green.*

23

floor out and dug?" he asked.

Green humored his request and the excavation proceeded, but not without consequences. With the next heavy rain, the entire structure collapsed and fell in the hole.

Through four decades, Smitty searched and searched again, his enthusiasm bolstered by occasional "finds." After one exhausting dig in the old cistern, he unearthed a corn cob pipe, a boot heel, and one other item, a dipper handle.

"He said the dipper handle was *very* significant," related Green.

But Smitty failed to appreciate a number of greenish rocks that his laborers hoisted from yet another hole. He was so unimpressed, in fact, that he left them lying on the ground when he departed for home, but as soon as he discussed the matter with a friend in Odessa, his eyes went wide.

"Smitty, don't you know what those were?" the person asked. "Them was emeralds."

That very night, Smitty drove the two hundred fifty miles back to the site, only to find the rocks gone.

Although he was never fated to uncover any actual jewels taken in a Comanche raid, his great-grandmother's tale may have served a greater purpose. "I think it was the search that was important for Mr. Smith," Green reflected in 2007. "I don't know whether he really expected to find anything or not, but he sure liked to look."

Ultimately, a seismograph truck pulled up to Green's home and one of Smitty's former diggers climbed out. Only then did the rancher learn that the old treasure hunter had died, though the spirit of the search lived on. Lest there be doubt, the man asked to investigate the old homestead area with sophisticated equipment that might, at last, reveal the underground void and its riches.

The succeeding two-day quest failed as miserably as a thousand holes stretching across forty years.

Nevertheless, Green came to believe that Smitty's account of his great-grandmother's girlhood among Comanches was not a total fabrication. "I asked one time whatever happened to that big ruby of hers, and he was very evasive," Green noted. "But there was enough element of truth woven into his story that made it interesting." Assuredly, Smitty had once pointed out an oak tree near the dugout and told him that the unmarked grave of a five-year-old girl lay beside it; when Green later made independent inquiry, a knowledgeable pioneer corroborated every detail.

Maybe history, not folklore, indeed graced the words of an old woman with an antelope-hide map in her hand and the gleam of a quail egg-sized ruby still in her eye. ★

Comanche chief Quanah Parker.
Library of Congress.

SEVEN HAUNTED JACK LOADS

Where a headless horseman rides the Texas night, a bonanza may not be far away.

Indeed, legend charges that Spaniards were wont to bury a dead man with a treasure so that his ghost would guard the site. If so, can any seeker hope to keep his head when those about him are losing theirs?

Perhaps a swath of rolling prairie near Denton Creek along the Denton-Wise county line could serve as a test of a treasure hunter's nerve, for not one, but *two* headless riders are said to

$1.25 million in gold bullion stacked in a bank in 1906. *Library of Congress.*

sentinel seven jack loads of hidden Spanish gold. Whether the cargo was ore, bullion, or coin is as unknown as its origin; tale-tellers say only that it was bound for the Gulf Coast through dangerous Indian country.

But this Spanish party had more than an Indian band skulking in its dust; a white man also followed, lured by the glittering riches. He watched the Spaniards as they dug a great hole throughout an entire day and night, and when morning broke, the ground was smooth again and the men rode away with seven unencumbered jacks. He didn't realize that their actions had been prompted by an imminent siege by Indians, and the gold seemed his for the taking. Then the war party swooped down and massacred the Spaniards, and it was all he could do to escape with his scalp and a golden memory.

In the early 1800s, he came back and began to sink a hole along Denton Creek south of present-day Stony community. He kept up the dig for the rest of his life, always sure that the gold was just one shovelful of dirt away, but he died with palms as empty as the excavation.

"That hole's still here—you could put a house in it," noted Bill Marquis of Stony in 2007.

When Oather Yeatts purchased the property in 1942, he was too concerned with farming prospects to worry about supposed treasure. But when a Mexican man showed up one day and asked to dig, he didn't deny the request. The Mexican proceeded to back away a half-mile from the nineteenth-century hole and took aim at the inside of Yeatts's pig pen, where he erected rigging for a bail bucket and set to work in the muddy mess with pick and shovel.

You danged fool, Yeatts thought.

By noon when the landowner broke from chores for lunch, the Mexican had gouged a pit seven feet deep. Yeatts didn't check again until evening, and this time he found him working by lantern light at the bottom of a hole deep enough to stack one man atop another. Fascinated by the Mexican's determination, Yeatts stayed and watched as he unearthed a spur with a rowel as large as a coffee can lid.

Evidently satisfied, the Mexican climbed out and began shoveling dirt into the hole. With the show over, Yeatts retired for the night, and by morning the excavation was filled and the man had left, never to return.

In the detective work that sometimes is the treasure hunter's life, a clue found in one place can sometimes lead to another, and so it may have been in the matter of the pig pen dig. Whether or not the spur directed the Mexican to the so-called "Money Hole" just across the Wise County line is not known, but this deep pit long has been rumored to hold Spanish gold—perhaps the very seven jack loads buried against the threat of Indian attack.

The site has had a less-than-romantic history, considering its reputation as a repository for festering cattle carcasses, rusting pickup trucks, and other refuse. But for a period of weeks around the turn of the twentieth century, it was the focus of an ambitious quest that spawned an incident worthy of Sleepy Hollow.

Bruce Lee had been born in 1896 and was still a mere boy, but he joined his father and a half dozen other men in a dig to unearth the Money Hole's secrets. They were convinced that its depths hid gold, for the gulf yawned unnaturally in solid rock, and only something of great value would have induced men to sink it.

For almost three weeks the seekers held their post, excavating by day and resting by night. Soon, perhaps the next morning, they would hoist the last barrel of dirt from the bottom and bare a gilded mass. With their excitement mounting, they slept only fitfully that final night and awoke before daylight to the drum of hoofs.

Bruce sat up with his father and the other men. Horses were fast approaching through an eerie darkness that made him shudder. What in the world . . .

Two horsemen emerged from the shadows, two *headless* horsemen, and between their ghostly mounts they dragged a chain. They seemed bound for the great mound of excavated dirt and the pit beyond. One rider passed to the left, the other to the right, and the chain swept a layer of earth back into the hole. Again and again the horsemen made a sally, each time returning more dirt from where it had come, until finally the pit of mystery was filled to its previous level and the headless riders disappeared into the night.

Within six months, every man who had tested the Money Hole spirits was dead. Young Bruce alone survived, and in the twilight of his eighty-nine years he related the story to Bill Marquis.

"I wouldn't laugh at him—everybody else would," Marquis remembered in 2007. "This man was so serious when he told this story."

Maybe, just maybe, Bruce Lee had good reason to be. Maybe he had been spared to carry a warning to a succeeding generation that the seven jack loads of Spanish gold were cursed and never to be disturbed. ★

THE GOLDEN HOARD OF JOSEPH SIMPKINS

Of all buried treasures, homestead caches have the greatest ring of authenticity. What was a pioneer settler to do in a near-wilderness without banks, other than conceal his life savings somewhere on his property?

Pity the unlucky family whose provider shared its location with no one and carried the secret to a sudden grave, as did Joseph Simpkins of East Texas in the 1860s.

Joseph was born in Wake County, North Carolina, in the 1790s; census records are contradictory as to the exact year. His wife also had North Carolina roots, having been christened Nancy (Stephens, likely) about 1810 in Lenoir County not far from the Atlantic coast. Sometime after their marriage, probably on June 7, 1824 in nearby Cumberland County, the couple emigrated to Walker County, Alabama, then Yalobusha County, Mississippi, and possibly to other states before settling in the Republic of Texas in 1843. A gunsmith by trade, Joseph also had farming and ranching aspirations and eyed the inviting country sixty-seven miles east of fledgling Dallas. Here a few miles north of the Sabine River in the republic's northeast sector, the land gently billowed and supported post oak and blackjack oak, as well as stirrup-high grasses that promised fat cattle and good herd increase. Furthermore, the sandy soil was ideal for dry land cotton farming, especially in light of a growing season of almost two hundred fifty days and an annual rainfall of more than forty inches.

Appearing before land commissioners in Rusk County in 1845 in accordance with an 1843 Republic of Texas congressional act, Joseph applied for and received an unconditional grant to six hundred forty acres. He proceeded to mark its boundaries along the current Wood-Rains county line, the area that so appealed to him, and the Simpkins ranch took root. A community known as Simpkins Prairie (present day Alba) eventually would rise up from the portion of his holdings in today's western Wood County.

As his family grew to include four children—Susan, Polly, Ellen, and John Edward Perlis Simpkins—Joseph built an empire of considerable proportions in what became the State of Texas. By September 1855 he held title to 1,360 acres, comprising his original grant, another 320 Wood County acres which he described as "my old place" near Lake Fork of the Sabine, and 400 acres in neighboring Hopkins County which he had acquired through transfer of a headright certificate. Furthermore, he burned his brand into 325 stock cattle, eighteen horses, and a mule. Helping with the chores, which also entailed cotton farming and hog raising, were two slaves: nineteen-year-old Venay, who had a child of eighteen months, and sixteen-year-old Ben, who was fated to play an important role in the Alba treasure legend.

In an era in which many people relied on subsistence farming for survival, Joseph Simpkins was wealthy.

A strong family tradition contends that Joseph followed suit with the prevailing practice and buried his liquid assets—a fortune in gold cradled in the sandy soil of a sprawling ranch thicketed by oaks. He kept the location even from his wife and children, for the walls sometimes had ears even in a sparsely settled frontier. As later events would suggest, however, he may not have been as secretive as he had thought.

By the end of the 1850s, Joseph's gold cache may have grown, for he had liquidated his 400 acres in Hopkins County and diverted full attention to maintaining his presence in Wood County, which now had a population of 3,963 whites and 923 slaves. In 1860 he duly paid taxes on his original 640-acre grant, as well as on another 320 Wood County acres.

With conflict threatening to rend the nation in early 1861, a vote for the secession of Texas passed with a 70 percent majority in Wood County. On April 12, war erupted at Fort Sumter, South Carolina, but no evidence exists that Joseph enlisted in the Confederate Army. Indeed, his face carried the creases of at least sixty-three years and as many as seventy-one, hardly

John Edward Perlis Simpkins, far left, at a gathering on Joseph Simpkins' 640-acre land grant. *Courtesy Saundra Burge.*

ideal for a soldier in a time when a man was old at forty-five. Nevertheless, he still had the energy and initiative to undertake an extraordinary venture—a cattle drive that involved not only his own beeves, but those of other ranchers in the area.

Exactly when Joseph said goodbye to Nancy and their children and set out in the dust of thousands of flinty hoofs is unclear, but it may have been before Wood County officials assessed taxes for 1861; the last roll bearing his name was 1860. Likely, his departure was prior to the first shots at Fort Sumter, for his probable course, the Shawnee Trail that pushed north through Dallas, was virtually abandoned during the war. At any rate, the trace carried him across the Red River near Preston, up through Indian Territory to Fort Gibson, and on into Kansas. Near the site where Coffeyville would be founded in 1869, tragedy struck.

"Joseph Simpkins," related his granddaughter-in-law Mamie Lowrie on May 15, 1935, "was killed by a horse. They always said he ought not to have been at the work he was at, because he was too old."

A variant tradition, passed along by Joseph's great-granddaughter, maintains that Joseph died in a fall from a wagon; perhaps a horse kicked him in the head as he struck the ground. Either way, his grave was just as shallow and the loss just as great.

As his fellow cowhands rode back down the long trail to Wood County to deliver the sad report to Nancy and their children, they had no inkling that Joseph had bequeathed to Texas a lost treasure that would endure into the twenty-first century. One can only imagine the impact the news had on his family that day, but Joseph's death was not lost on his slaves either, and what happened that very night   has fueled speculation among his descendants for a century and a half.

His longtime slave Ben, now in his early twenties, ran away, never to be seen again.

The questions loom immense. Had Ben seen Joseph at his cache? Did this young black man with little hope for a future claim his master's gold and flee to start a new life?

Perhaps, perhaps not, but as Nancy and her children searched the property, they found not a shovelful of upturned dirt to suggest that Joseph's gold had been robbed. The reassurance benefited them little, though, for neither did they find a single clue pointing to the cache.

Mamie Lowrie.
Courtesy Saundra Burge.

For generations, Joseph Simpkins' treasure has been the object of obsessive quests.

"My grandmother [born in 1894] said she could remember seeing lights over in the woods when she was a child—they were digging for his money," related Joseph's great-great-great-granddaughter, Saundra Burge, in 2007. "Even we have looked. My son walked the creek banks with a metal detector. My grandkids or my brother would walk over in the back pasture and look. I can remember the old-timers around Alba all wondering, 'What happened to Joseph's money?'"

Indeed, what did happen to this lost hoard of gold bought at the price of a man's sudden death?

Only field and woods and a century past know the answer, and they aren't talking. And neither are the descendants of a runaway slave. ★

THE GOLD OF THE BESIEGED

Common details can stud treasure legends like identical diamonds in a crown. Coupled with the sheer number of such tales, might this suggest the unthinkable to scoffers—a basis in fact?

Consider a pair of yarns that color the folklore of Nolan and Fisher counties. In one account, two men cross the area with two pack horses heavily loaded with gold ingots. The second story identifies the venturers as Spanish wagoners; their number is uncertain, but they too carry bars of gold.

Each tale holds that Indians besiege the party, inducing the men to bury their payload. In the first narrative, the Spaniards sketch a map of its location before falling prey to the scalp knives. In the second, the treasure's existence comes to light through testimony of a survivor who draws a map for a friend from his deathbed in El Paso.

"When you hear a story over and over and over and it stays about the same," observed veteran treasure hunter Bill Marquis of Denton County, "there's a pretty good chance there's something to it."

A common thread so binds the stories in Fisher and Nolan that entire lives have been devoted to establishing its veracity—and the only way to do so is by unearthing a treasure lost.

Two sites along the Fisher-Nolan county line have come under particular scrutiny. One is along winding Sweetwater Creek near Eskota, founded in 1881 as a cattle shipping point on the Texas and Pacific Railway in southeast Fisher County.

Settlers in this bottomland evidently were unaware that their community shielded a legend, but all of that changed when a stranger showed up one day with a breathtaking story. He was the very individual, he claimed, who had received the deathbed map in El Paso; furthermore, the map pointed straight to these bends of Sweetwater Creek.

After identifying an exact location, he hired two Sweetwater men and put them to work. They dug, and dug some more, until the excavation reached extraordinary depth, and when townspeople asked why anyone under siege by Indians would have buried riches at such a level, he explained that they hadn't.

"Gold is heavy," he told them, "and it keeps a-sinkin.'"

Even after striking water he persisted, pumping the hole dry. Finally he slunk away, broken by failure, but other seekers followed in his wake and sank holes of their own.

Eskota was a town of fifty people, a store, and a church when forty-one-year-old Roland Kinsey purchased the adjacent 123-acre plat dotted with excavations in 1947, and soon his younger cousin Walton Kinsey moved to the site and took up the search. On a trip to Mexico, Walton purchased a treasure map that eerily paralleled the lay of the land at Eskota. Not only did it show the horseshoe bend of Sweetwater Creek, but also the red rock bluff that fronted it and a large pecan tree with which he was familiar. Excited, he tested the waybill soon after returning home.

As instructed, he pressed his back against the pecan's south side and looked down the line of a huge limb stretching southwest. He paced off the requisite number of steps in that direction, turned, and faced east. The map showed something

Walton Kinsey. *Courtesy Walton Kinsey.*

"unnatural" ahead, and the red rock cliff seemed to fit the description. Again, he stepped off the indicated number of paces, then stopped where X marked the spot. He couldn't help but take note that the original excavation of many years' past lay fifty to one hundred feet from his map's starting point at the big pecan.

Anyway, Walton began to dig, checking the pit every so often with his metal detector. "Boy, it was just a-singin' like everything," he remembered decades later. "I got down there and I found a complete buggy axle. But when I moved it and all the rust, the metal detector didn't show anything else."

It was Walton's first dry hole, but it wouldn't be his last. Even after deciding his map was a fake, he kept up the search.

Once, he discovered a human skeleton, largely intact except for the skull, in a sloughed bank at the nearby confluence of Sweetwater Creek and a tributary. With the remains were part of a Springfield rifle and an aluminum medallion emblazoned with a star and the name "W. H. Chandler," fueling speculation that the grave might be associated with the Indian attack of legend. Despite inquiries, he was never able to establish a connection.

By 2007, Eskota was a ghost town and Walton was almost eighty, but he continued to prowl Sweetwater Creek in quest of a myth. "I guess I do it for a pastime," he reflected.

Another cousin, Ronnie Kinsey, eventually inherited the property but never succumbed to the treasure's allure, although in 2007 he admitted to digging a twelve-foot pit with a backhoe one afternoon. "I'm just not one of those that know you're going to get rich digging buried treasure," he said.

It was a lesson not learned nine miles east on the Nolan-Fisher county line, where hundreds of holes stretching across decades demonstrated man's willingness to chase a rainbow's end. Like a magnet acting upon metal, the coils of Kildoogan Creek just north of Sweetwater have drawn seekers ever since a Mexican man reportedly hired on with a nearby farm sometime in the foggy past. Between chores, he babbled about besieged Spanish wagoners burying gold in this very dirt, and when his bosses laughed, he produced a frazzled half of a parchment map that he had received from a previous landowner to whom he was related. How the prior farmer had gained possession of the parchment is unclear; perhaps it had surfaced in a furrow.

Regardless, it pointed to treasure, and the search was on, limited only by financial backing for caterpillars and dynamite.

Howard Whitworth dug, supposedly guided by this map or another handed down by his father, but had only blisters to show when he sold the property to Ed Freeze. Freeze dug, gaining more blisters, then in the late 1960s he accepted the help of Onesimo M. Jacques, a Sweetwater man with a facility for smooth talk and salesmanship.

Onesimo M. Jacques. *Courtesy Rodney Jacques.*

"He had a mouth on him that could sell anything," his son Rodney remembered in 2007.

Born in 1923, the elder Jacques had worked as a hay baler, combine operator, and fencing contractor, but now he had a new passion in treasure hunting. With his gift of gab, he enlisted the services of a series of temporary shareholders with equipment that ranged from the ordinary to the bizarre. Holes born of jackhammers or backhoes soon dotted the terrain like

The dig for gold proceeds. *Courtesy Rodney Jacques.*

doughnut mounds in a prairie dog town, as various individuals with electronic devices, seismic trucks, or witching tools pointed the way. One man plopped down on an instrument

Ed Freeze inspects dig. *Courtesy Rodney Jacques.*

that resembled a toilet seat; another set in motion a "knotter ball." Shaped like a large egg and dangling by a string from a support, the "male" knotter ball would act in opposition to a "female" knotter ball which the Spaniards supposedly had buried with the treasure.

"It would start back and forth kind of like a pendulum and do the cross," recalled Rodney, a participant in his father's venture. "We looked like gophers, making holes all over the place. They finally gave up on that one."

No less diverse than the myriad devices were the individuals solicited by his father—among them an oceanic treasure hunter reputed to have been featured in *National Geographic,* and a mysterious bearded man in his late forties. Even Jacques didn't know his name; he soon dubbed him "Mainer" for his main role in bringing in financing and heavy equipment.

"This man was always hiding," remembered Rodney. "If he'd see a car for any length of time behind him, he'd get all nervous, like somebody was always after him."

Ed Freeze working on shaft. *Courtesy Rodney Jacques.*

At one point, a Fisher County man showed up with the very section of ragged parchment which the long-ago Mexican farm hand had displayed. Although it constituted only half a waybill, it had much to say to the initiated.

"The map," recalled Rodney, who was among those who studied it, "had to be folded on the corners in a special way, then it would show something like turtles and what they called twin mountains."

The double hills were visible on the western horizon, but the men didn't know what to make of the turtles until they uncovered a concrete-like rock in the shape of one. Still, a large portion of the map remained missing and the quest went on.

Across more than two decades the digs persisted, with the ground yielding little more than water and prehistoric vertebrae. Then in the early 1990s, Jacques and his latest out-of-town partners engineered the project's most ambitious shaft yet.

"The thing was so deep we couldn't see the bottom of it because of the shadows," recalled Rodney.

Onesimo M. Jacques in an empty treasure dig.
Courtesy Rodney Jacques.

Always the last one off the property, the elder Jacques locked the gate one evening and went home, but as the night wore on, he sensed something amiss and returned with his son. To their confusion, a fresh excavation several feet wide marked the shaft's upper level.

Onesimo M. Jacques and Ed Freeze search for a bonanza. *Courtesy Rodney Jacques.*

They sped to the Sweetwater motel where their partners lodged, only to find that they unaccountably had checked out, leaving suitcases behind in their haste. In light of the expanded dig, Jacques and his son could only assume the worst—the men had struck gold and skipped out.

Still, Jacques couldn't be sure, and all he could do was study the parchment map and start another hole. Now, new shareholders entered the picture, and an innocuous search for treasure turned as threatening as the Indian fight that had spawned it.

"It was like a Mafia coming in—they had machine guns and everything," related Rodney. "Even my dad had his gun."

With gold fever raging and gunplay only a twitch of a trigger finger away, trouble was inevitable. One day when a neighbor took issue with the operation and fired shots over their heads, the Mafioso-types whirled and the gunfight was on. Luckily, every bullet whizzed astray, but it took all of Jacques's slick talk and peacemaking skills to quell the violence.

The incident marked the end of Jacques's long and obsessive search, and when he died at age seventy-eight in 2001, his palms were still as bare as the holes that men had sunk for generations at two sites of promised treasure nine miles apart. Hypnotic yet elusive, this gold born of blood seems destined to tempt and taunt as long as there are seekers undaunted by past failures. ★

Onesimo M. Jacques watches a backhoe dig for Spanish gold.
Courtesy Rodney Jacques.

THE GOLDEN CALF

A fabulous bonanza is the treasure hunter's Promised Land. But like Moses, most will wander a lifetime for nothing more than perhaps a fleeting glimpse from afar.

The average person would not guess that the Delaware Indians figure prominently in a Texas tale of treasure seen and lost, but the informed would be less surprised to learn that this legend associates a Delaware band with the Hebrews at Mount Sinai. Indeed, the Delawares were so receptive to Christian tenets that long-ago treaties sometimes referred to them as "Christian Indians."

Like the descendants of Abraham, the Delawares embarked on a soul-searching exodus that carried them across a wilderness. When Europeans first arrived on the Atlantic coast, they found 20,000 Indians entrenched in present day New York, New Jersey, Delaware, and Pennsylvania and referred to the tribe by the name of the Delaware basin where they lived. The Indians preferred the designation *Lenape,* Algonquin for "True Men." Normally a peaceful people, they welcomed Christian missionaries who sought to convert them from their native religion. Their first contact with Christianity came in 1643, when Lutheran clergyman Johann Campanius began a five-year crusade near a Swedish settlement in current Delaware. Still, another century would pass before the faith began to impact the tribe significantly.

In Pennsylvania in the 1740s, Delawares opened their villages to Moravian missionaries, zealous Protestants who preached Christ, pacifism, and temperance. As European and American demand for land forced the Delawares farther west over the next century, Moravians went with them. Although the missionaries gained many converts, *Lenape* culture was so inseparable from traditional *Lenape* religion that the tribe's practice of Christianity was sometimes a blend of the old and the new. Delawares embraced the idea of an afterlife, for example, but discarded the orthodox Christian concept of heaven and hell.

About 1820, a band of Missouri *Lenape* known as the Absentee Delawares migrated to northeast Texas and entered into friendly relations with peoples of this Spanish and later Mexican province. When the Republic of Texas declared independence in 1836, the new government sought the tribe's support, although no treaty was ever ratified. Under the presidency of Sam Houston, Delawares were employed as scouts for Texas Rangers patrolling the western frontier, and it was probably during this time that a band of sixty-five Delawares led by Jim Ned settled in what is now Wise County.

The peaceful co-existence promoted by Houston was not fated to endure. When Mirabeau B. Lamar became president in 1838, he ordered all immigrant Indians, including Delawares, expelled into Indian Territory. Between the Cherokee War of 1839 and Houston's second term as president in the early 1840s, *Lenapes* trod the Texas landscape only at their peril.

Now, legend enters the story. One party of Delawares chose to stay in what is now northeast Wise County rather than cross the Red River into Indian Territory. After all, this region near later Greenwood community marked the end of a 1500-

mile, 100-year exodus from their ancestors' homeland in the Delaware basin. The parallels with the Hebrews' flight from Egypt and subsequent forty years of wandering were not lost on them. This band's Mount Sinai lay in these live oak hills with their sparkling streams and plentiful game, and it was here that they had done as the Hebrews had done—fashioned a golden calf that they could worship.

Four Texans evidently saw the smoke of their campfires and went to investigate. Bellying up to the top of a ridge, they looked down on a scene right out of the Old Testament, for the Delawares were paying homage to an idol of gold. Astounded, the four men retained the presence of mind to recognize in the

Nicolas Poussin's seventeenth-century *Adoration of the Golden Calf*.

band a threat and went for help. Returning with a larger force, they killed every Indian and turned their attention to seizing the golden calf—but where was it?

They searched the camp, the oaks, the hills, the streams, but the Delawares had concealed their idol well.

Across a century and a half, the mystery of this passing glance at a wondrous treasure has endured, luring seekers such as Bill Marquis of adjacent Denton County. "I'd heard this when I was a little kid," the sixty-two-year-old noted in 2007. "I always thought, 'Well, that's a bunch of bull—there wasn't no Delaware Indians in this country.' Well, I found out that there were. People supposedly hunted for that golden calf forever all over that country."

Perhaps, though, there is a reason that the land still refuses to yield its secret. Could the Delawares have ground the golden calf into powder and drunk it as their Hebrew counterparts had done? ★

A BALL OF SILVER

Born a lowly slave before the Civil War, he lived more than a century to cast a sizable shadow over the legendry of hidden treasure in North Texas.

The modern era has lost track of his name, but not the folktale—a story of loss that gives men reason to set forth on a quest. All the wonderment and allure took root in the 1850s, when a resolute Texan helped settle the stream-graced prairie near present-day Ponder in Denton County. His two slaves, a man and his young son, thought highly of the kindly settler and chose to stay with him even after the government granted their freedom. As the pioneer neared death, he bequeathed his farm to the only family he had: his onetime slaves.

A bonanza in silver. *Photo-illustration by Richard Galle.*

The inheritance also brought the blacks cash, but even as banks started up in nearby Denton, father and son did as their

51

former master and concealed it around their homestead. Even after the father died, the son kept up the practice, continually adding to the hoard throughout his working years. His vault of choice was his barn, where he kept paper money buried in a bucket. In a corner, meanwhile, silver coins accumulated across two centuries until they filled a fifty-five-gallon wooden barrel—the ultimate in piggy banks.

Despite his prosperity, the former slave never purchased an auto, preferring a rickety, horse-drawn wagon that regularly creaked to Denton and back as late as the mid twentieth century.

"I remember him vaguely from when I was a kid," said Texas Slim, a colorful treasure hunter who asked that his real name be withheld. "I never had anything to do with him, but I thought it was neat he still drove a wagon and horse."

In the 1960s, the ex-slave gained a reputation as more than an eccentric; at 109 years of age, he was said to be the oldest man in the nation. Then disaster struck—his barn burned to the ground. Even as he stirred the ashes, he could no longer pinpoint his buried money cache; furthermore, the thousands of silver coins had melted and assumed the shape of the barrel.

Shaken, he wrote a letter to an Oklahoma insurance company, which may have held a policy on the barn. "I have had a great loss, amounting to over $80,000," he said.

No one knows how much of that total had been in paper and how much in silver, but if he based his coinage loss strictly on face value—as he undoubtedly did—the barrel-shaped mass would eventually reach the proportions of a small fortune. By September 2006, a single old-style silver dollar had appreciated ten-fold on the basis of its silver content alone.

Perhaps seeking to exchange the recast silver for paper money, the old gent loaded it in the wagon bed and the vehicle rumbled into Ponder. Several years later, Texas Slim heard a description of his cargo from the local blacksmith.

"He said this big ball of silver covered the whole back of the wagon," Slim related. "It had melted, and there was whole coins stuck all in it."

Exactly what the ex-slave did with his unusual freight is a matter of conjecture. "What *would* you do with a ball of silver?" the blacksmith later wondered. "I guess he carried it back home."

Most wagon loads of gold or silver were heavily guarded, as in this 1890 shipment of $250,000 in gold bullion. *Library of Congress*.

Soon the old man died, and the mystery of the silver's whereabouts began to spice the conversations of Ponder old-timers. Slim, after corroborating the blacksmith's account with two other people in the 1970s, romanced the idea that the former slave's humble rock house harbored treasure. One Halloween, he slipped in with his metal detector.

"People had tore the floor up, they'd tore the walls out, looking for money," Slim remembered in 2007. "But I did find a letter that talked about his loss amounting to over $80,000."

Turning his attention to a search for the old barn site, he located a concentration of charred nails in an area thirty feet wide and forty feet long. Drawn to the southwest corner by his metal detector, he unearthed an old lard bucket that held a treasure hunter's dream, albeit a modest one.

"There was coins in the bottom of the can, and there was folded paper money on top," he recalled. "It was just coming all to pieces."

The find was extraordinary on one level, but on another it only added to the intrigue. A bank managed to salvage $286 in bills, and the remaining crumbles couldn't possibly have constituted $80,000. Regardless of how the old gent had figured his losses, it was clear that the argentine mass cast by fire had comprised far more silver dollars than anyone had ever suspected.

So what *would* a person do with a barrel-shaped mold of pure silver large enough to fill a wagon bed?

The answer rests only in the realm of legend—and in the mind of a man born a slave and shaped by 109 years of experiences. ★

BLOOD MONEY ON THE SOUTH PLAINS

Pioneer emigrants were seldom rich, yet reputed lost treasures dust the very trails they chased toward western dreams. Whether along famed Texas traces such as the Lower or Upper roads of 1849, or upon unnamed routes still undated, fleeting gold or wispy silver always seemed to mark

The dry bed of Salt Lake in Midland County in 2008.
Courtesy Richard Galle.

wagons' passage.

In present Midland County, two natural lakes testify to the ghosts of emigrants past and bonanzas perhaps concealed.

Salt Lake sinks into the lower South Plains ten miles southeast of Midland and forms a gulf a quarter-mile wide and a mile long. White-splashed with mineral deposits, the lake bed has its own drainage basin that deluges it with fresh water during heavy rainfall. In early days, the lake supported fish and nurtured so many fowls that in 1906 one observer dubbed it "the greatest duck resort in the West."

The value of such an oasis was not lost on nineteenth-century emigrants who braved this uncharted route to the Pecos River, seventy-five miles to the west. They camped just west of the lake's south end, hunted its shores, and filled their water barrels for the push into the sunset.

Sometime before the Civil War, according to legend, the ordinary demands of survival turned extraordinary for members of a large wagon train bearing fabulous wealth. Setting up camp at the lake, they fell prey to an attack by Indians. As the siege persisted and hopes dimmed, the emigrants buried the riches for safekeeping. A single man eluded massacre and fled with not only horrid memories but sole knowledge of the treasure's whereabouts—information he withheld until his deathbed.

Whether or not the man was delusional in his final moments was debatable, but the nightmarish scene that a U.S. Cavalry detachment soon rode upon at Salt Lake was all too real, at least in folklore. Strewn on the southwest bank were one hundred fifty human skeletons, a literal valley of dry bones silently crying out the truth of the dead man's tale. Caring individuals, likely the soldiers themselves, buried the remains, and although the graves' location soon passed from memory, on into the twentieth century wagon irons and half-burned planks memorialized a one-time emigrant presence here. By 1906, treasure hunters already had combed the lake time and again, sinking hole after empty hole—but the quest was only beginning.

By the 1930s, Herd Midkiff (1897-1971) gained familiarity with the site through his salt-collecting operation to benefit his nearby ranch. "I remember him talking about people coming out and looking for gold," recalled his son, Bob Midkiff.

"I was just a kid whenever I first heard of [the search]," said another of Herd's sons, John Midkiff, who was born in 1932. "There's lots of people hunted for gold down there. I'd hear of it occasionally through the years, but then it finally faded."

When young Richard Galle and his teenaged brother ventured to Salt Lake about 1956, they were unaware of the story of massacre and a treasure hidden. Their search was for arrowheads, and as they scoured the lake's southwest shore, they stumbled on an incredible find.

"There were all sorts of little rivulets or washouts that were maybe two feet across and three, four feet deep," recalled the younger Galle. "We were just jumping over those when my brother said, 'Stop! There's a rattlesnake down there!'"

Halting, the brothers noticed an unusual detail about the rivulet.

"There were three kind of earthen bridges across this two-foot expanse," Galle continued. "There was space underneath where the water would run through. Something was holding the earth together there."

Digging into the formations, the youths were startled to discover apparent graves.

"In all three of them there were bones—they appeared to be human bones," Galle related. "It seems like we pulled out a radius or ulna, the forearm bones. Presumably, the bones were kind of the glue that kept the bridge together."

Whether or not the graves represented the mass burial of legend—and thus offered partial corroboration of a buried

William G. Chaney at the Parks Ranch lake in the mid-1950s. *Courtesy Weldon Chaney.*

fortune—no one can say. Still, the Galle brothers had established not only that death had visited the lake, but that gravediggers had plunged their shovels into the very southwestern point that, in folklore, had served as brood grounds for a massacre.

Ten miles southwest of Salt Lake, along a direct wagon course to Emigrant Crossing on the Pecos, another basin also has raised men's hopes of a big strike. Only a mile or so north of this unnamed lake, which sparkled like a jewel in the elevated barrens of Parks Ranch in the mid-1930s, William G. Chaney worked a Great Depression farm of 320 acres. West of the Chaney place unfurled a second farm that also bordered the Parks outfit, and one day a stranger assumed occupancy with the apparent intent of eking out a hardscrabble living in soil fit only for grass burrs. Noting his inexperience, Chaney befriended the stranger and earned his respect.

Still, Chaney could only scratch his head as he dwelled on matters. "This guy is going to starve to death over there," he told his wife Virgie. "He knows absolutely nothing about farming. Besides that, he doesn't really work at it."

One night, Virgie noticed an unusual beam of light among the nearby knolls that cradled the lake. "Somebody's doing something up there with a lantern," she charged the next day, "and I don't understand it."

Initially, Chaney dismissed the light as a reflection, and even when she pointed out the lantern glow to the entire family one evening, he paid it little thought.

"He's probably just hunting," he offered. "The guy's kind of a nut anyway. Just forget it."

In the middle of a subsequent black night, the man showed

up at Chaney's isolated home and roused him from bed.

"I'm leaving—I'm out of here—I'm gone," the man told him in private. "You've been good to me and treated me fair and I want to do something for you."

The man proceeded to bequeath to Chaney his crops and anything else of value on his farm.

"I've got everything I need to supply me for the rest of my life," the man explained. "Up there on that hill—and I've marked the spot for you—there's plenty of valuables. You need to go up there and seek that out. There's a big rock under the ground and you've got to get around that rock. When you do this, it'll be rewarding to you. I'm fixed for life, so you go."

The man disappeared into the night, and a couple of days later Chaney inspected a flagged area at the lake and discovered excavations and a disinterred iron pot. Clearly, the man had used his farming operation as a ruse to conduct an unauthorized treasure search on adjacent Parks land.

Smitten, Chaney enlisted the aid of his seventeen-year-old farm hand in his own secretive dig. Sinking a shaft by grubbing hoe and shovel, they struck a backbreaking rock as described, but soon abandoned the tenuous promise of unsubstantiated riches for the solid assurance of modest fields.

Still intrigued a dozen or so years later, Chaney returned by night to a basin now bone-dry to experiment with an M-Scope, the latest in metal-detecting equipment.

"In this dry lake bed we got a really big reaction," recalled his son Weldon, a teenager at the time. "We dug down six or eight or ten feet and hit the bottom of the lake bed. The ground was hard as table top. Ultimately, we got some dynamite and we

Weldon Chaney and his brother, William G. Chaney Jr., at the Chaney homestead in the 1930s. *Courtesy Weldon Chaney.*

drilled some holes. We tried to loosen up that soil under there, but didn't have any luck."

Even as they concealed all evidence of their excavation, father and son planned to return someday with landowner permission and the next generation of equipment. Sidetracked by quests for other rainbows' ends, however, they never resumed their investigation of this lake that may have shielded a cache whose origin was lost even to folklore. Nevertheless, on into the twenty-first century the mystery haunted Weldon as he considered that long-ago night when a neighboring tenant had shaken his father out of bed.

"This guy knew something," Weldon reflected. "He found something. He came and told my dad. Evidence was there. This is not conjecture, speculation, a wives' tale—this is fact."

Facts, though, seldom seem to direct a seeker to a golden dream, leading some observers to ponder a vital question. Do buried treasures reveal themselves only to individuals so predestined?

Whether at a lake perhaps bloodied by emigrant massacre or at a watering point another day's travel southwest, the answer may confirm the notion by which crusty old prospectors have always sworn: *Gold is where you find it.* ★

THE SANTIAGO PEAK CACHE

A mountain of majesty and mystery, 6,524-foot Santiago Peak guards secrets as vast as the wasteland that kneels before it.

Santiago Peak. *Courtesy Richard Galle.*

Across the Chihuahuan Desert slithers the serrated backbone of the Santiago chain, a serpent in its own hell. Two-thirds of the way along its thirty-eight-mile snake track, from Dog Canyon in Big Bend National Park to Del Norte Gap on the northwest, the monarch of this barren range rises 3,000 vertical feet, an imposing landmark for motorists southbound from Marathon on U.S. 385 and from Alpine on Texas 118. Indeed, Santiago Peak's truncated apex not only dominates the horizon from many far-flung points in the Big Bend, it long has stood in defiance against any who seek to tame it or solve its riddles.

The foundation of its reported treasure rests somewhere in the past, but even the origin of its name lies in the realm of fanciful thought. *Viejos* of the Big Bend used to say that Don Santiago, a Chisos Apache chief of the late seventeenth century, lent his name to the peak after riding a bloody trail across New Spain's northern frontier. When Spanish troops led by Juan Fernandez de Retana finally trapped the raiders on a mountain height south of the Rio Grande in 1693, Santiago fought back fiercely before surrendering.

A second Indian chief named Santiago, whose heyday was approximately the 1870s, also came to be identified with the mountain. He and his band frequently traded, gambled, and liquored up well south of the Rio Grande in San Carlos, whose citizens were wary but not intimidated by his reputation for trouble. When Santiago's traders finally turned into raiders and rode north with captive girls, townspeople took up the trail. Across moonscape and through mountain defile, the Mexicans kept up the chase, finally overtaking the warriors before they reached the Rio Grande. Still, Santiago refused to surrender his spoils, and a running skirmish ensued all the way into the Big Bend. One by one the Indians fell, until Santiago alone remained to escape in the night.

At daybreak the Mexicans resumed pursuit, tracking him ever closer to the jutting mountain now known as Santiago Peak. When dusk found the avengers about to surround him at its base, Santiago abandoned his exhausted horse and scrambled up the steep, rocky slope. As hard dark fell, the Mexicans could only listen as he taunted them from the sky with the cry "*Soy Santiago!* I am Santiago!"

By sunup, he had disappeared, but not before giving his name to the mountain, claim some.

A third Indian chief, of an unidentified tribe, also burned his mark into Santiago Peak legendry. In 1905 an octogenarian fiddler, who folklore remembers only as "Uncle Worthy," related details of an 1870s skirmish between Texas Rangers and Indians in broken country in Santiago Peak's very shadow. In camp with Company G, Worthy sat roasting venison over a fire when a rifle slug ripped through his right ear. Whirling, he heard the answering blast of a Ranger's Springfield in the recesses of an arroyo. Soon, the captain came riding up "with his Springfield a-smokin'" and announced that he had felled the shooter, a chief. The body, the captain added later, was to be left undisturbed as a warning for the remaining raiders.

Daring to refuse the order, Worthy took vengeance: an ear for an ear. Secretly whacking off the chief's right appendage, he dropped it inside his fiddle, where it still remained three decades later.

This unnamed chief, along with Santiago of the San Carlos raid and the earlier Don Santiago, gave rise to a legend still in vogue in the twenty-first century—that "Chief Santiago" lies buried on Santiago Peak's lofty summit.

Some tale-tellers, however, hold that the peak is not the namesake of an Indian but rather of one of Jesus's twelve disciples, Santiago, also known as James, the son of Zebedee. As patron saint of the military Order of Santiago, he was ever on the minds of Spanish soldiers, who shouted his name as they engaged an enemy. It was under such circumstances that the battle cry *"Santiago!"* echoed from the mountain's battlement about 1750. As a small Spanish military unit encountered an overwhelming force of Indians near its foot, the soldiers' spirits sank until their commander pointed to the wisps that obscured the summit like the host of heaven.

"Even now," he cried, "Santiago may be watching from the clouds on yonder mountain!"

Encouraged, the soldiers shouted their patron saint's name and routed the hostiles.

Yet another figure who may have inspired the peak's appellation was the Mexican Santiago of Presidio del Norte, situated across the Rio Grande from present day Presidio. In the mid nineteenth century or earlier, the fearless Santiago led the fight against marauding Apaches and Comanches, whom he pursued with a vengeance back toward their *rancherias* in Texas. When a small party of raiders struck Presidio del Norte again one night and made off with horses, Santiago and five other men took up the trail.

For a day the tracks led east toward the Chisos, then veered north in the direction of a mighty, flat-topped mountain yet unnamed. As evening fell on the fourth day, Santiago ordered a halt under the looming peak and dispatched a pair of scouts to seek out the Indians' camp. Successful, the men returned to lead a daybreak assault on the raiders' stronghold. Opening fire, the Mexicans killed three of the Indians and scattered the others, only to come under counterattack. Charged by a mounted warrior, Santiago held his ground and fired, even as his companions fled. Santiago's bullet missed, but a slug from the Indian's firearm exploded through his hips and knocked him from his horse, leaving him defenseless as the warrior rode up and recognized him.

"Santiago," demanded the Indian before administering the coup de grace, "why do you cry, when you have killed three of our side, while you have lost only one of your own?"

The Mexicans buried Santiago there—some say at the mountain's base, others say on its summit—and piled rocks over a grave that had no need for an etched headstone, for henceforth the very peak would bear his name.

With the completion of the intercontinental Southern Pacific Railroad twenty-seven miles north of the mountain in 1883, settlement of the area began in earnest. Promoters and land speculators swarmed the region in search of a fast buck, laying out town sites and selling lots to distant parties. Some developers were legitimate; others were outright frauds. With no swamp land in West Texas to dump on unwary buyers, John L. Mauk and Lee R. Davis turned to Brewster County and Santiago Peak in a classic land scam of all land scams. The two Waco men acquired the mountain from William Poole and, with his blessing, organized Progress City Town Site Company by the close of 1909. On January 3, 1910, Mauk and Davis filed a map of Progress City with the Brewster County Clerk's office.

Incredibly, the town site lay on the very summit of virtually unassailable Santiago Peak.

Before authorities got wise to the scheme, the company had sold more than a thousand small lots for generally $1.50 apiece to gullible buyers who purchased sight unseen from distant regions of the state. On February 8, 1910, a Brewster County grand jury reported the swindle to district court judge W. C. Douglas in Alpine. Not only was so-called Progress City "accessible only by horseback and then along a difficult and little used trail," said the jury, but Santiago Peak was "totally uninhabited and uninhabitable, and wholly unfit for . . . a town. In fact, the land is . . . of no use whatever except that of grazing livestock."

Nevertheless, for decades thereafter, uninformed lot owners would venture to Brewster County to check on their investments.

When thirty-year-old rancher Will G. "Bill" Gulihur of Barnhart ventured to Brewster in search of range land in 1920, county officials told him that a two-section ranch encompassing Santiago Peak was available for the cost of the unpaid back taxes. For a mere $600 in 1921, Gulihur acquired a legendary refuge of lost riches and, with the aid of a surveyor, set about staking off its unfenced boundaries. Grazing was sparse and water was limited to a seasonal spring, but Gulihur saw enough promise to build a box house and bring out his wife Emma, their four children, two hundred fifty goats, twenty cattle, and ten horses.

For a while, Gulihur hauled water from a nearby ranch, then imported a drilling rig with the aid of eight burros and sank an unreliable well. Soon, a windmill whirred in the desert breeze and pumped gyppy stock water into a tank.

Will and Emma Gulihur. *Courtesy Rowdy Shackelford.*

The Gulihur box house. *Courtesy Rowdy Shackelford.*

The homestead wasn't Progress City, but at least Gulihur was making progress.

Goats, and later sheep, were not deterred by Santiago Peak's treacherous heights, which dramatically thrust skyward more than 1,500 feet from an upper plateau at the limits of horse travel. Roundups forced Gulihur, his son Fred, his grandsons, and Mexican herders to extreme measures; they scaled the mountain hand-over-foot and traversed its steep slopes in high-wire fashion.

"We'd go up the north side," related Rowdy Shackelford, a grandson born in 1930. "We'd get up there so far and somebody would stop, then another fellow

Rowdy Shackelford, horseback, and Fred Gulihur on the ranch in the early 1930s. *Courtesy Rowdy Shackelford.*

and another one would stop. Somebody had to go right on top. He'd holler at the others . . . and we'd just start going around [the mountain] to drive everything off to the

Rowdy Shackelford at age 77. *Courtesy Rowdy Shackelford.*

bottom. And we'd [circle] right on around to where we started. All I done was just walk around the edge and keep the sheep and goats pushed off to the next man. There'd be one or two

Rowdy Shackelford in the Santiago Peak country.
Courtesy Jerry Gulihur.

who would stay down in the bottom to go around horseback. Then we'd go down, pick up our horses, and join the herd."

It was demanding work, but it served to familiarize Gulihur and his family with Santiago Peak and its heretofore hidden crest. They found the summit generally flat and somewhat oblong, with a 300-yard east rim and grassland that unfurled toward a western point 600 yards distant. There, overlooking the sunset, the twentieth century was about to meet legend, for a pile of rocks provided unmistakable evidence of a long-ago grave.

Gulihur and a compadre later decided to learn the truth about fabled Chief Santiago and came back with a pick and a shovel. As the exhumation wore on, Gulihur paused to take stock of the matter and studied his friend.

"Say," he asked, "what are you going to do if that Indian chief suddenly jumps out of this hole we're diggin' and says, 'What the heck y'all doin' here, anyway?'"

It was all the discouragement his superstitious friend needed. "Aw, let's quit," he suggested. "I didn't want to dig him up anyway."

In the 1930s, however, Gulihur's son Fred and a man named Cot Meeks resumed the dig, uncovering a human skull but no artifacts that might identify the remains as one of the Chiefs Santiago or the Mexican Santiago of Presidio del Norte. Nevertheless, they retained the skull as they clambered down the slope to their waiting mounts. Years later, Fred Gulihur related to his son the details of what ensued.

"They got on their horses and rode back to the house," remembered Jerry Gulihur, who was raised on the Santiago Peak ranch from his birth in 1940 until 1950. "Cot had this skull on his saddle horn like it was looking

Nine-year-old Jerry Gulihur at Santiago Peak Ranch headquarters in 1949. *Courtesy Jerry Gulihur.*

out ahead. My mother walked out there and got mad at him: 'Get rid of it! What are you doing with that thing!' They both laughed, but [my father] got rid of it."

The mountain's most romantic mystery, however, is a hidden cache of Spanish coins whose origin is lost to folklore as well as to history. Yet of all supposed buried treasures in Texas, this is one of the few that yielded tangible evidence of its existence; indeed, in 2007 a reliable witness could still recall seeing one of the coins in his father's palm.

For Fred Gulihur, the intrigue started when a goat herder showed up with a burro one day in the early 1930s and asked for a job. Fred, in his twenties and taking an active role in ranch affairs, had met the man before; for the past year the Mexican national had herded goats for the nearby YE Mesa outfit. The 5,385-foot YE tableland, roughly circular with a diameter of just under two miles, rose more than 2,000 feet from the desert floor a mere four miles southeast of Santiago Peak.

"I was working for the wrong hombre," contended the goat

Goats leaving windmill on the Santiago Peak Ranch.
Courtesy Rowdy Shackelford.

73

herder with a glance at Santiago Peak. "I need to be up *here*."

Fred already had a herder on the payroll, but Santiago's rugged expanses demanded a greater presence and he hired the newcomer. Rather than join his comrade in the existing backcountry camp, the Mexican strangely asked to set up stakes at Spanish Oak Mott on the peak's northeast side. Here in a 3,800-foot canyon, a wet weather spring gave birth to a half-acre of dense brush, an oasis in a land otherwise generally barren.

Fred had no reason to deny the request, and soon the new herder was roaming the hidden fastness of the Santiago Peak area with the flock. On a regular basis, Fred made rounds of the two camps by horseback, checking on the men's welfare and delivering sacks of flour and other supplies. A few months after hiring the second herder, the rancher rode up to Spanish Oak Mott to find goats scattered and the camp abandoned;

Fred Gulihur on "Ranger" at Santiago Peak
Ranch headquarters in 1944. *Courtesy Jerry Gulihur.*

furthermore, flour covered the ground as if the Mexican had poured it out to make other use of the sacks, which were missing. Climbing off his horse and investigating, Fred uncovered an astounding piece of evidence—an old Spanish silver coin.

Riding back to the homestead, he related the goat herder's bizarre disappearance and displayed the coin. "This was laying there where he must've dropped it when he was loading his stuff on a burro," he said. "Then he just left out afoot."

The puzzle persisted until Fred hired another laborer from the same region of Mexico and told him of the incident a year or so later. To the rancher's astonishment, this new employee not only knew the goat herder, but claimed that the missing man had returned to his home village with a vast treasure in Spanish coins hauled in flour sacks.

It had not been a chance find, noted the informant. Indeed, the goat herder had come to the Santiago Peak area for the very purpose of seeking out a cache to which a family member had directed him. The treasure's origin was not known; perhaps he had drawn upon a long-standing family tradition with roots in the Spanish era. Initially, he had believed it to lie on YE Mesa, which explained his service herding YE goats, but later he had determined that the money rested on or near Santiago Peak.

Now, a new question began to haunt Fred Gulihur: Had the goat herder made off with the entire cache or tapped only a part?

Returning to Spanish Oak Mott, he searched the gulch and surrounding bluffs for a sign—maybe an empty hole or shallow cave—but Santiago Peak only laughed a mute laugh of derision. Still, as word of the treasure spread, other seekers became convinced that the goat herder had taken only as much silver as his burro could carry and had concealed the rest. In subsequent years, treasure hunters repeatedly showed up at the ranch and asked Fred's permission to search.

"Go look for it," he would tell them. "I've been all over that outfit, and I hadn't ever found nothing."

The seekers would proceed to scour the mountain and canyons before abandoning their quest and driving away in a trail of dust. Watching them depart, Fred would only shake his head.

"Ain't nobody," he would soliloquize, "found nothing yet."

Nevertheless, the piece of silver from Spanish Oak Mott bore testimony that the treasure was real.

"I remember

Jerry Gulihur in 1966. *Courtesy Jerry Gulihur.*

76

Macky Shackelford, Rowdy Shackelford, and Jerry Gulihur in the Santiago Mountains. *Courtesy Jerry Gulihur.*

that one coin," his son Jerry Gulihur recalled in 2007. "Daddy had it around for a while. I was just a little ol' kid. I don't know what ever happened to that, but he used to show it to people."

The Spanish cache still remained elusive when the Gulihurs sold Santiago Peak in 1950, but in the ensuing decades a clue to its location, or of another such bonanza on or near the mountain, arose in the folklore of the Big Bend. Find a turtle etched into a rock, say the raconteurs, and you will have found where "Santiago and his outlaws" buried a great treasure; perhaps this is the "Chief Santiago" who plundered San Carlos, Mexico, and escaped pursuers at Santiago Peak.

In the early 1990s, two deer hunters did not concern themselves with sorting out such details when they got lost in impenetrable fog in the Santiago Peak country. In fact, they were oblivious to the legend and wanted only to find their way out of the mountains. The mist persisted for days as the men wandered aimlessly, lugging their rifles and sometimes pausing to take ghostly pictures with a camera.

One such snapshot was of a turtle carved into a rock.

Finally the fog lifted and the hunters staggered back to safety, the unwitting holders of visual evidence of a vital treasure marker. Only after they developed the film and sent the ranch foreman a set of pictures did they learn that they had stumbled upon a site possibly harboring long-lost wealth.

Searching their memories for its location, they recalled nothing but dense mist that had clouded every landmark and had cast them into utter confusion, rendering it impossible to retrace their steps.

As wild and sovereign as ever, Santiago Peak, like many other Texas citadels of treasure lost, seems destined to hold fast its enigmas for a generation yet unborn. ★

WHERE I DUG FOR BURIED TREASURE

Interviews

Batteas, Lester; Sweetwater – 30 November 2007.

Boner, Hubert; Bowie – 3 December 2007.

Boner, Lois; Bowie – 3 December 2007.

Booth, Geraldine; Mahomet – 18 January 2008.

Bunch, Jody; Burnet – 4 December 2007.

Burge, Saundra; Alba – 30 November 2007.

Chaney, Weldon; Midland – 21 March 1995.

Clower, Kerry; Alvord – 3 December 2007.

Galle, Richard; Midland – 8 December 2007.

Goble, Carole; Burnet – 4 December 2007.

Goble, Perry; Burnet – 4 December 2007.

Green, Bob; Albany – 1 December 2007.

Gregg, Rosalie; Decatur – 3 December 2007.

Gulihur, Jerry; Alpine – 15 December 2007.

Jackson, Mike; Sunset – 3 and 14 December 2007.

Jacques, Rodney; Sweetwater – 1 December 2007.

Kinsey, Ronnie; Sweetwater – 30 November 2007.

Kinsey, Walton; Sweetwater – 30 November 2007.

Lee, Maisie; Marathon – 14 December 2007.

Marquis, Bill; Denton County – 5 December 2007.

Midkiff, Bob; Midland – 5 and 8 December 2007.

Midkiff, John; Midland – 6 December 2007.

Morrison, Jeanette; Dallas, 4 December 2007.

Nutt, Waymond; San Antonio, 4 December 2007.

Payne, Scott; Decatur, 5 December 2007.

Price, Willie Mae; McAllen, 18 January 2008.

Roberts, Ike; Marathon, 14 December 2007.

Rooney, Shirley; Marathon, 15 December 2007.

Shackelford, Macky; Marathon, 15 December 2007.

Shackelford, Marilyn; Marathon, 15 December 2007.

Shackelford, Rowdy; San Angelo, 15 December 2007.

Shugart, Clifford; Phoenix, Arizona, 4 December 2007.

Sisk, David; Denton, 4 December 2007.

Sisk, Evelyn; Bowie, 3 December 2007.

Books

Fulcher, Walter. *The Way I Heard It: Tales of the Big Bend*.
　　Austin: University of Texas Press, 1959.

Madison, Virginia. *The Big Bend Country of Texas*.
　　Albuquerque: University of New Mexico
　　Press, 1955.

_____ and Stillwell, Hallie. *How Come It's Called That?: Place
　　Names in the Big Bend Country*.
　　New York: October House Inc., rev. ed. 1968.

Myres, S.D. *Pioneer Surveyor, Frontier Lawyer: The Personal
　　Narrative of O.W. Williams 1877–1902*.
　　El Paso: Texas Western College Press, 1966.

The New Handbook of Texas, Volumes 1–6. Austin: The Texas
　　State Historical Association, 1996.

Tyler, Ron C. *The Big Bend: A History of the Last Texas
　　Frontier*. College Station: Texas A&M
　　University Press, 1996.

Patrick Dearen. *Courtesy Richard Galle.*

Recognized by *Southwestern Historical Quarterly* as a "worthy successor to J. Frank Dobie," Patrick Dearen has researched lost treasures of Texas for more than twenty-five years. His book *Castle Gap and the Pecos Frontier* broke new ground in the study of hidden bonanzas in the state's western reaches. The author of nine novels and eight nonfiction books, Dearen has been honored by Western Writers of America, West Texas Historical Association, and Permian Historical Association. He makes his home in Midland, Texas. ★

Lone Star Lost
Buried Treasures in Texas

ISBN 978-0-87565-392-1
Case. $9.95

A TEXAS SMALL BOOK
★

ISBN 978-0-87565-392-1

9 780875 653921   50995